# GREAT GRANNY

by Ann Bryant and Barbara Szepesi Szucs

## FRANKLIN WATTS
### LONDON • SYDNEY

# CHAPTER 1

Miss Rudge's class was learning all about
the Second World War. Jake liked listening to
Miss Rudge telling the children what life was like
when their grandparents were children.
He enjoyed hearing about the soldiers and
the places they had been. But his friend, Ryan,
didn't like the lessons – he said they were boring.

Second World War

One day, Jake's great grandmother came to collect him from school. Jake loved going to her house because she always told him such interesting and exciting stories about when she was young.

Miss Rudge made her way through the parents and children and came over to talk to Great Granny. "The children are learning all about the Second World War. We'd love you to talk to them about it," she said.

"Oh no!" said Ryan. "Not more about the war. That's going to be so boring."

Jake felt quite cross. "Great Granny won't be boring. She tells brilliant stories!" he said.

# CHAPTER 2

After tea, Great Granny went to her computer

in the study. Jake went too. While she was typing,

Jake used a pile of books to build a plane.

He had a great time pretending to be a pilot

while Great Granny was busy.

"What are you writing?" Jake asked.

"Is it for when you come into school?"

Granny nodded and kept typing on her computer.

When she had finished, she looked up and smiled

at Jake. "Actually," she said, "I am writing a book."

"Wow!" said Jake. "What's it about?"

"You'll see!" said Great Granny, her eyes twinkling.

8

On her desk there was a photo of Great Grandad. In the photo, Jake was sitting on his lap. Jake had been just a baby when the photo was taken. Grandad was wearing a silver chain that looked a bit like a necklace. Jake wondered where the chain was now. He couldn't remember ever having seen it.

# CHAPTER 3

The next day Great Granny came into Jake's
class to talk about the Second World War. She
told the children how women didn't go to war
to fight but they did other important jobs.
Some women worked on farms and in factories.
Great Granny told the class she had been
a nurse.

"Now I'm going to tell you all a story," said Great Granny. "It is about a brave pilot. One day during the war, there was a terrible air raid. A plane dropped from the sky when the enemy shot at it."

A few of the children gasped.

"The plane was on fire," Great Granny went on, "and it landed in the sea. But the pilot was trapped inside the cockpit."

"Oh no!" Miss Rudge exclaimed.

Jake wondered what was going to happen to the poor pilot. He might die because of the fire.

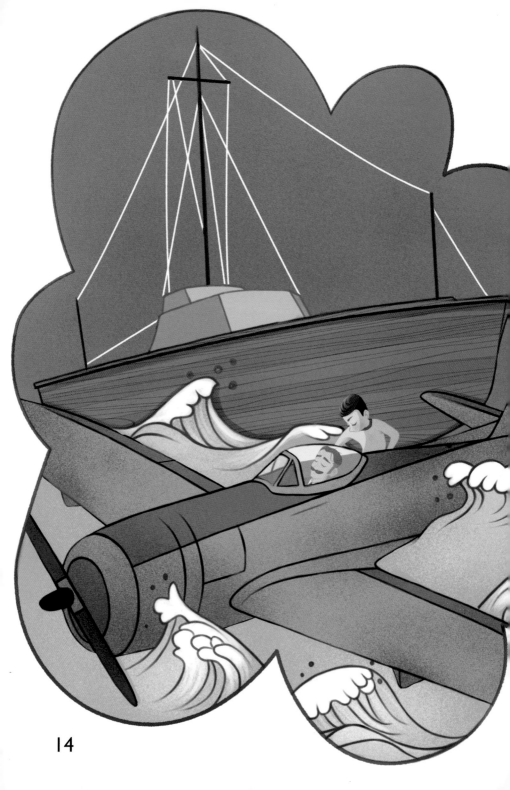

"There was a rescue ship nearby," Great Granny explained. "There were many men trapped in the water calling for help. The rescue team came up to the pilot. He was so still and quiet they thought he must be dead, so they went off to help the others. But one rescuer stayed behind," Great Granny went on. "He stayed in the freezing cold sea and worked until he managed to free the pilot."

"Then what happened?" asked Miss Rudge, in a soft voice.

"Well," said Great Granny, "the pilot was taken straight to hospital where the nurses would be able to take good care of him."

"So he was alive!" Ryan called out.

"Yes," smiled Great Granny.

Great Granny held up the photo of Jake

sitting on Great Grandad's lap, wearing

the silver chain.

"This is Jake's great grandad," said Great Granny.

"He was the pilot in my story. He risked his own

life on a secret flying mission during the war.

He was on his way back to base when he

got shot down."

Second World War

Great Grandma's voice went quiet. "But when he came ashore, after being rescued, he couldn't move at all. I was there when the men were getting him into the ambulance. I could tell there wasn't time to take him to hospital. He might have died on the way. But luckily I was a nurse and I knew what to do to make him better."

# CHAPTER 4

Did you help save his life?" asked Ryan.

"Yes I did," replied Great Granny.

"And later, when he was better,

we got married."

Jake saw that Miss Rudge had a tear in her eye.

And when he looked round the class he saw that

all the children were wide-eyed with wonder and

amazement.

"You were very brave," said one of the girls.

"Yes and so was Jake's great grandad,"

someone else said.

Everyone talked about how brave both of Jake's

great grandparents were.

"The medal that Jake is wearing in the photo is very special," said Great Granny.

"It's the medal Jake's great grandfather got from the prime minister at the end of the war.

Here it is. I have kept it safe

for all these years."

Jake felt really proud of Great Granny. He'd only just realised that the silver chain in the photo was a medal. But now he realised something else. He jumped to his feet. "My great granny is writing a book on her computer all about what happened!" he said.

Great Granny smiled at Jake. "That's right," she said. "It's the story of Jake's great grandad."

"I love hearing about the Second World War now," whispered Ryan to Jake. "And you know what? Your great granny really is great!"

# Things to think about

1. Why is Ryan not looking forward to hearing Jake's great granny give a talk?
2. How does Jake feel about his great granny coming to school? Why?
3. What effect does Great Granny's story have on the class?
4. What did Great Granny do during the war?
5. How did Great Granny help in the pilot's rescue?

# Write it yourself

One of the themes in this story is changing an opinion. Now try to write your own story about a similar theme.

Plan your story before you begin to write it.
Start off with a story map:
• a beginning to introduce the characters and where your story is set (the setting);
• a problem that the main characters will need to fix in the story;
• an ending where the problems are resolved.

Get writing! Try to add some dramatic events such as "the plane was on fire." to describe your story world and excite your reader.

# Notes for parents and carers

## Independent reading

The aim of independent reading is to read this book with ease. This series is designed to provide an opportunity for your child to read for pleasure and enjoyment. These notes are written for you to help your child make the most of this book.

## About the book

Jake's great granny has lots of exciting stories to tell, but his friend Ryan thinks all old people are boring. When Great Granny comes to the school to give a talk, Jake can't wait. He knows her tales about survival and rescue in the Second World War will have his class – including Ryan– gripped!

## Before reading

Ask your child why they have selected this book. Look at the title and blurb together. What do they think it will be about? Do they think they will like it?

## During reading

Encourage your child to read independently. If they get stuck on a longer word, remind them that they can find syllable chunks that can be sounded out from left to right. They can also read on in the sentence and think about what would make sense.

## After reading

Support comprehension by talking about the story. What happened?
Then help your child think about the messages in the book that go beyond the story, using the questions on the page opposite. Give your child a chance to respond to the story, asking:
Did you enjoy the story and why?
Who was your favourite character?

Franklin Watts
First published in Great Britain in 2018
by The Watts Publishing Group

Series Editors: Jackie Hamley and Melanie Palmer
Series Advisors: Dr Sue Bodman and Glen Franklin
Series Designer: Peter Scoulding

A CIP catalogue record for this book is
available from the British Library.

ISBN 978 1 4451 6310 9 (hbk)
ISBN 978 1 4451 6312 3 (pbk)
ISBN 978 1 4451 6311 6 (library ebook)

Printed in China

Franklin Watts
An imprint of
Hachette Children's Group
Part of The Watts Publishing Group
Carmelite House
50 Victoria Embankment
London EC4Y 0DZ

An Hachette UK Company
www.hachette.co.uk

www.franklinwatts.co.uk